40 do's and don'ts while in prison

40 do's and don'ts while in prison

Kenqua Smith

Kenqua Smith
40 DO'S AND DON'TS WHILE IN PRISON

Published by Spines Publishing Platform
ISBN: 979-8-89569-369-8

contents

one
borrowing money

IN PRISON, managing your finances can be a tricky endeavor. Borrowing money from other inmates is a common occurrence, but it can lead to a whole host of problems if not handled carefully. Here are some do's and don'ts to keep in mind when it comes to borrowing money behind bars.

Do's:

1. Only borrow money from individuals you trust: When seeking financial assistance from fellow inmates, make sure you are borrowing from someone you have a good relationship with. Trust is crucial in such transactions.
2. Clearly establish repayment terms: Before accepting any money, discuss and agree upon the terms of repayment. Be honest about when and how you will return the borrowed funds.
3. Keep track of borrowed amounts: Maintain a record of all borrowed money to avoid confusion or disputes later on. This will help you stay accountable and organised.

4. Prioritize repayment: Make repaying any debts a priority. By honoring your financial commitments promptly, you build credibility and trust within the prison community.
5. Do not Seek help, if you're unable to repay: If you find yourself unable to fulfill your repayment obligations, Do not seek assistance from any other inmates; Being transparent about your financial struggles can help prevent potential conflicts.

Don'ts:

1. Borrow from questionable sources: Avoid borrowing money from individuals with a reputation for violence or deceit. It's essential to protect yourself from potential harm or exploitation.
2. Borrow more than you can repay: Be cautious not to borrow beyond your means. Taking on excessive debt can lead to a cycle of financial instability and strain your relationships.
3. Ignore repayment deadlines: Respect the agreed-upon repayment schedule and deadlines. Failing to do so can damage your credibility and jeopardize future financial transactions.
4. Rely solely on borrowing: While borrowing money can be a temporary solution, it's essential to explore other avenues for managing your finances, such as earning through work opportunities or participating in prison activities.
5. Engage in borrowing for non-essential items: Avoid borrowing money for unnecessary or frivolous purchases. Focus on meeting your basic needs and essential expenses before considering discretionary spending.

By following these do's and don'ts when it comes to borrowing money in prison, you can navigate financial transactions more effectively and maintain positive relationships within the inmate community. Remember, financial integrity and responsibility are key aspects of thriving in a prison environment.

two
witnessing violence

IN A PRISON ENVIRONMENT, witnessing violence can be a terrifying and traumatic experience. It's crucial to know how to navigate such situations to protect yourself and maintain your safety. Here are some important guidelines to keep in mind when it comes to witnessing violence in prison.

1. **Stay Calm**: The first and most crucial step when witnessing violence is to stay calm. Panicking or reacting impulsively can escalate the situation and put yourself at risk.
2. **Assess the Situation**: Before taking any action, assess the situation carefully. Determine if there is an immediate threat to your safety or if you can remove yourself from the situation without intervening.
3. **Avoid Direct Involvement**: While it may be tempting to step in and try to stop the violence, it's essential to understand your limitations. Directly involving yourself in a violent altercation can put you in harm's way.
4. **Do Not Seek Help**: Although, witnessing violence in prison can be a terrible and traumatic experience, it's

important to 'not seek help' from correctional officers or other authorities. Reporting the incident can make your own time in prison very harmful for you (even to the point of death), and almost certainly ensure that the individuals involved, will seek to exact violence upon you as well.

5. While, seeking help from correctional officers or other authorities, is prison policy and the humane thing to do. Prisoners see, seeking help or reporting things like this to the authorities, as 'snitching or ratting,' and both are frowned upon by inmates. **Maintain Distance**: When witnessing violence, it's crucial to maintain a safe distance from the altercation. Avoid getting too close to the individuals involved to protect yourself from becoming a target.
6. **Do Not Instigate**:Under no circumstances should you instigate or provoke violence in a prison setting. Engaging in such behavior can have severe consequences and put your safety at risk.
7. **Do Not Observe and Report**: Remember your safety and life is on the line, never feel the urge to be a spectator and/or an instigator of the violence; hear no evil, see no evil is the way to go.
8. **Protect Yourself**: While witnessing violence, prioritize your safety above all else. If you feel threatened or in danger, seek refuge in a secure location until the situation is under control.
9. **Do Not try to help Victims of violence.**: If you witness violence towards another inmate, Do Not offer your support and assistance in a non-confrontational manner. Providing help and empathy can make a you look soft and like a 'do-gooder' to other inmates. Both are frown upon by prisoners.
10. **Familiarize yourself With the Prison's Rules and Inmate Rules**: While is helpful to learn the rules of

the prison, for handling violent incidents, so you don't break any prison rules and get into trouble for it. It is just as important to learn the 'Inmate Code' for your own safety and well-being as well.

Understanding the proper way to behave as an inmate between you and other inmates, can help maintain the trust and favor other inmates have towards you. By following these guidelines when witnessing violence in a prison setting, you can protect yourself, and give yourself a safety net, while in prison.

three
avoiding crowds

IN THE PRISON ENVIRONMENT, it's essential to navigate various social situations with caution and awareness. One important aspect to consider while serving time is the concept of avoiding crowds. Crowded spaces in prison can often lead to misunderstandings, conflicts, or even dangerous situations.

Here are some key points to keep in mind when it comes to handling crowds in a correctional facility. Firstly, it's crucial to be mindful of your surroundings and the people you are surrounded by in crowded areas. Avoid getting too close to groups that may be engaging in risky behavior or conflicts. By staying on the periphery of crowds and observing from a safe distance, you can better assess the situation and decide whether it's best to stay or leave.

Additionally, it's wise to avoid being drawn into large gatherings or activities that may have negative implications. Crowds can sometimes create a sense of anonymity, leading individuals to act in ways they wouldn't otherwise. By maintaining a level head and resisting peer pressure to join in on questionable activities, you can protect yourself from potential trouble.

Moreover, when navigating crowded spaces, it's essential to keep a low profile and avoid drawing unnecessary attention to yourself. Being discreet and keeping to yourself can help you steer clear of unwanted interactions or conflicts that may arise within groups of inmates. Furthermore, if you find yourself in a situation where a crowd is forming around a potentially volatile incident, it's best to remove yourself from the area as quickly and calmly as possible. Avoid getting caught up in the commotion or being perceived as part of the problem by association.

Overall, when it comes to avoiding crowds in prison, the key is to stay vigilant, maintain your composure, and make strategic decisions about your interactions and surroundings. By being mindful of your environment and exercising caution in crowded situations, you can better protect yourself and navigate the complexities of prison life more effectively.

four
consequences of snitching

CONSEQUENCES OF SNITCHING When serving time in prison, one must be acutely aware of the consequences of snitching. Snitching, also known as informing or ratting, refers to the act of providing information to authorities or prison staff about the activities of other inmates.

While some may see it as a way to gain favor or protection, the repercussions of snitching can be severe and long-lasting. Snitching is considered a serious violation of the inmate code, often resulting in ostracism, violence, or even death. In the tightly-knit community of a prison, trust is paramount, and those who are perceived as betraying that trust by snitching are met with hostility and retaliation. Inmates rely on each other for support and protection, and any breach of this trust is met with swift and harsh consequences.

Furthermore, snitching can have legal implications, leading to potential charges of being a "snitch" or a "rat." In the prison environment, being labeled as a snitch can make one a target for retribution from other inmates, putting their safety at risk.

Additionally, prison authorities may view snitches as untrustworthy and unreliable, affecting any potential for early release or privileges. It is crucial to understand that the consequences of snitching extend far beyond the immediate moment. Even if one believes they are providing information for the greater good or their own benefit, the repercussions can be long-lasting and detrimental to their well-being in prison and beyond. Snitching can lead to a loss of respect, trust, and safety within the prison community, making it vital to weigh the potential consequences before considering such actions. In conclusion, the consequences of snitching in prison are severe and can have lasting impacts on an inmate's safety, well-being, and reputation.

It is essential to understand the gravity of this action and consider the potential ramifications before engaging in any form of informing on fellow inmates. Building trust and maintaining integrity within the prison community are crucial for survival and navigating the challenges of serving time behind bars.

five
keeping your word

IN A PLACE LIKE PRISON, where trust and integrity are of utmost importance, one of the key principles to abide by is keeping your word. Your word is your bond, and it holds significant weight in the inmate community. Failing to keep your word can have serious repercussions, damaging your reputation and potentially putting you in harm's way.

When you make a promise or commitment to someone in prison, whether it's a favor, a trade, or any form of agreement, it is essential to follow through. Breaking your word not only reflects poorly on your character but also erodes the trust others have in you. In a confined environment like prison, where relationships and alliances play a crucial role in your safety and well-being, maintaining your integrity is vital.

Keeping your word is not just about fulfilling promises; it's also about being honest and transparent in your interactions with others. If circumstances change and you are unable to uphold your end of the deal, it is important to communicate this openly and honestly. People in prison value sincerity and honesty, even if it means admitting that you cannot fulfil a commitment you made.

Furthermore, keeping your word extends beyond just individual agreements. It also involves respecting the rules and regulations set by prison authorities. By following the guidelines and abiding by the established protocols, you demonstrate your commitment to being a responsible and trustworthy inmate. In a place where loyalty and honor are valued commodities, your ability to keep your word can make a significant impact on how you are perceived by your fellow inmates.

By honoring your commitments, you not only build a reputation for reliability but also earn the respect and trust of those around you. In conclusion, keeping your word is a fundamental principle that should guide your actions and decisions while serving time in prison. By upholding your promises, being truthful, and following through on your commitments, you not only protect your integrity but also contribute to a positive and trustworthy environment within the prison community.

Remember, in a place where words carry weight, your ability to keep your word can make a world of difference in how you navigate the challenges of prison life.

six

navigating inmates

NAVIGATING Inmates Navigating the social dynamics within a prison environment can be challenging, but with the right approach, you can navigate through interactions with other inmates successfully. Here are some important points to consider when it comes to interacting with fellow prisoners:

1. **Borrowing Money**: It's best to avoid borrowing money in prison if possible. Debts can lead to conflicts and put you in a vulnerable position.
2. **Witnessing Violence**: If you witness violence, it's important to respect the 'inmate code' on this matter, and stay out of it and clear of it. DO NOT involve yourself or inform the prison authorities; it will only put your own safety in jeopardy.
3. **Avoiding Crowds**: Large crowds can sometimes lead to tension and conflicts. Try to avoid getting caught up in crowded areas to minimize the risk of confrontation.
4. **Consequences of Snitching**: Snitching can have severe repercussions in a prison setting. It's crucial to

weigh the risks before deciding to share information with the authorities.

5. **Keeping Your Word**: Building trust among inmates is essential. Always strive to keep your word and follow through on promises to maintain credibility.
6. **Reciprocating Favors**: If someone does you a favor, make sure to reciprocate when the opportunity arises. Building positive relationships through mutual support is key.
7. **Drugs and Tattoos**: Avoid getting involved with drugs or tattoos in prison. Engaging in such activities can lead to serious consequences and jeopardize your safety.
8. **Interacting with Others**: Treat fellow inmates with respect and courtesy. Establishing positive relationships based on mutual respect can help create a safer environment for everyone.
9. **Maintaining Silence**: Sometimes, it's best to keep to yourself and avoid unnecessary conversations or conflicts. Maintaining a level of silence can help you stay out of trouble.
10. **Avoiding Gambling**: Gambling can lead to debts and conflicts. It's advisable to steer clear of gambling activities to prevent potential confrontations.
11. **Securing Belongings**: Keep your personal belongings secure to avoid theft or disputes over property. Staying organized and mindful of your possessions can help prevent unnecessary conflicts.
12. **Being Wary of Predators**: Be cautious of individuals who may try to take advantage of you. Trust your instincts and seek support from trusted individuals if you feel threatened.
13. **Building Trust**: Trust is a valuable currency in prison. Establishing trust with others through

honesty and reliability can help you navigate relationships more effectively.

14. **Self-Defense Strategies**: While avoiding conflicts is ideal, it's essential to have basic self-defense strategies in case of emergencies. Knowing how to protect yourself can be crucial for your safety.
15. **Protecting Legal Information**: Keep your legal information confidential and secure. Sharing sensitive details about your case can have serious consequences and compromise your legal defense. In a prison setting, understanding and navigating inmate interactions are essential for your safety and well-being.

By following these guidelines and being mindful of your actions, you can navigate the complexities of inmate relationships effectively.

seven
reciprocating favors

RECIPROCATING Favors In the microcosm of prison life, favors are currency. They establish relationships, build trust, and maintain a sense of camaraderie among inmates. However, the concept of reciprocating favors is not as straightforward as it may seem. It involves a delicate balance of give and take, trust and reliability. Here are some key points to keep in mind when navigating the intricacies of reciprocating favors behind bars.

Understand the Value of a Favor In prison, favors are not to be taken lightly. Whether it's lending a pack of cigarettes, sharing food, or helping with a chore, every favor carries significance. Before asking for or offering a favor, consider its weight and impact on both parties involved. Reciprocity is essential in maintaining healthy relationships in a confined environment.

Be Selective in Asking for Favors. While it's common to seek help from fellow inmates, be mindful of the frequency and nature of your requests. Constantly relying on others without reciprocating can strain relationships and create a sense of imbalance. Choose the favors wisely and be prepared to offer something in return when the time comes.

Keep Track of Favors Owed and Repaid to avoid misunderstandings and conflicts, it's crucial to keep a mental or written record of favors owed and repaid. This way, you can ensure that you fulfill your end of the bargain and hold others accountable for their commitments. Clear communication and transparency are key in maintaining a fair and respectful exchange of favors.

Avoid Manipulative Behavior Reciprocating favors should come from a place of genuine goodwill, not manipulation or coercion. Avoid using favors as leverage to gain power or control over others. Respect boundaries and never exploit someone's vulnerability or need for personal gain.

True exchange of favors, is based on mutual respect and trust. Express Gratitude and Appreciation, when someone extends a favor to you, always express your gratitude and appreciation. A simple thank you, can go a long way, in fostering positive relationships and building trust. Acknowledge the effort and kindness of others, and be ready to reciprocate when the opportunity arises.

In conclusion, reciprocating favors in prison is a nuanced practice that requires thoughtfulness, integrity, and respect. By understanding the value of favors, being selective in your requests, keeping track of exchanges, avoiding manipulative behavior, and expressing gratitude, you can navigate the complex dynamics of favor-sharing with grace and dignity. Remember, in the realm of reciprocating favors, what goes around comes around.

eight
drugs and tattoos

IN THE COMPLEX and often volatile environment of prison life, certain aspects require careful consideration to navigate successfully. One crucial factor to address is the presence of drugs and tattoos within the prison setting. Understanding the implications and consequences of involvement with drugs and tattoos is paramount to ensuring safety and well-being during incarceration.

Drugs are strictly prohibited within prisons for various reasons, including the potential for violence, addiction, and disruption of order. Inmates should steer clear of any involvement with drugs, whether it be possession, use, or distribution. The consequences of being caught with drugs can result in extended sentences, loss of privileges, and even placement in solitary confinement. Additionally, drug use can lead to physical and mental health issues, exacerbating an already challenging situation.

Tattoos, while not inherently illegal, can carry significant implications within the prison system. Inmates should be cautious when considering getting tattoos, as they can be associated with gang affiliations, criminal history, or other negative connotations. In some cases, tattoos may attract unwanted attention or put individuals at risk of conflict with other inmates. It is important to weigh the potential consequences of getting a tattoo and consider the long-term implications it may have on one's reputation and safety.

Furthermore, the process of obtaining tattoos in prison is often unsanitary and poses health risks such as infection or disease transmission. Inmates should prioritize their health and well-being by avoiding makeshift tattoo parlors and opting for safe and hygienic practices if they choose to get a tattoo. Overall, staying away from drugs and carefully considering the implications of tattoos are essential components of navigating the prison environment successfully.

By making informed choices and prioritizing personal safety and well-being, inmates can mitigate risks and focus on rehabilitation and eventual reintegration into society.

nine
interacting with others

NAVIGATING the complex social dynamics within a prison environment is crucial for your safety and well-being. Interacting with others can be both challenging and rewarding, but it's essential to navigate these relationships with caution and respect.

Here are some key points to consider when engaging with fellow inmates: Building Trust: Trust is a valuable commodity in prison. Be honest and reliable in your interactions with others to establish trust. Keep your word and follow through on promises to maintain credibility within the inmate community. Interacting with Others: Treat others with respect and kindness, regardless of their background or reputation. Showing empathy and understanding can go a long way in fostering positive relationships with your fellow inmates.

Reciprocating Favors: In prison, favors are often exchanged as a form of currency. If someone helps you out, be sure to reciprocate the favor when the opportunity arises. This not only builds goodwill but also ensures that you have a network of support when needed. Navigating Inmates: Be observant of the social hierarchy and dynamics among inmates.

Avoid getting involved in power struggles or conflicts that could put you in a dangerous position. Respect others' boundaries and be mindful of your interactions with different groups. Respecting Property: Respect others' personal space and belongings. Avoid touching or using items that do not belong to you without permission. Treat others' property with the same care and respect you would expect for your own.

Dealing with Theft: If you suspect that someone has stolen from you, address the issue calmly and discreetly. Avoid escalating the situation into a confrontation, as this could lead to further harm. Seek assistance from prison authorities if necessary. Rejecting Control: Do not allow others to manipulate or control you through fear or intimidation.

Stand up for yourself and assert your boundaries firmly but respectfully. Avoid getting involved in activities that compromise your values or beliefs. Protecting Privacy: Maintain a level of privacy in your interactions with others. Avoid sharing personal information or engaging in gossip that could be used against you.

Respect others' privacy as you would want them to respect yours. Intercepting Conversations: Be cautious when engaging in conversations that may involve sensitive or incriminating information. Avoid being drawn into discussions that could compromise your safety or legal standing. Exercise discretion and think before you speak.

Phone Etiquette: When using the phone, be mindful of others waiting to make calls. Keep your conversations brief and to the point, respecting the needs of fellow inmates. Avoid discussing sensitive topics or engaging in arguments while on the phone.

Handling Threats: If you receive threats from other inmates, DO NOT go report them to prison authorities. While reporting threats to the prison authorities, may be the policy of the prison. For your own safety and reputation, among the other inmates, you must always attempt to handle threats towards you, on your own. Seeking protection and support from prison staff to ensure your safety in prison, is considered weak and cowardly and not to be respected at all.

Observing Table Etiquette: When dining with others, practice good table manners and hygiene. Avoid talking with your mouth full, slurping food, or making loud noises that could disrupt others. Respect the shared space and be considerate of your fellow inmates. By following these guidelines, you can navigate the complexities of interacting with others in a prison environment while maintaining your safety and integrity.

Remember to treat others with respect, uphold your values, and stand your ground when needed.

ten
maintaining silence

IN THE COMPLEX and often dangerous environment of a prison, maintaining silence can be a crucial aspect of survival. Keeping your thoughts to yourself and being selective about what you share with others can help protect you from unnecessary conflicts, unwanted attention, and potential danger.

One of the key reasons to maintain silence in prison is to avoid getting involved in situations that may lead to trouble. By keeping a low profile and not drawing unnecessary attention to yourself, you can reduce the likelihood of being targeted by other inmates or getting caught up in disputes that could escalate quickly.

Furthermore, maintaining silence can also help you protect your privacy and personal information. In a setting where trust is hard to come by, being cautious about what you reveal about yourself can prevent others from taking advantage of you or using sensitive details against you.

Another important aspect of maintaining silence is to avoid getting entangled in gossip or rumors. By refraining from spreading information or engaging in conversations that are not relevant to you, you can steer clear of unnecessary drama and potential conflicts that could arise from misunderstandings or misinformation. It's essential to remember that silence doesn't mean isolation or cutting off all communication with others. You can still engage in meaningful conversations and build relationships while being mindful of what you share and with whom.

Developing a small circle of trusted individuals with whom you can confide can provide you with much-needed support and companionship without compromising your safety.

In conclusion, maintaining silence in prison is not about shutting yourself off from the world but rather about being strategic in your interactions and guarding your words carefully. By practicing discretion, avoiding unnecessary chatter, and being selective about who you trust, you can navigate the challenges of prison life more effectively and protect yourself from potential harm.

eleven
avoiding gambling

GAMBLING CAN BE a tempting pastime for many inmates in prison. The allure of making quick money or passing the time can be strong, but engaging in gambling activities can lead to serious consequences. It's important to remember the risks involved and make wise choices when it comes to avoiding gambling while serving time. In prison, gambling can often lead to disputes and conflicts among inmates. Money is a sensitive subject, and when stakes are involved, tensions can escalate quickly.

Avoiding gambling altogether is the best way to steer clear of unnecessary trouble. It's essential to prioritize your well-being and focus on productive activities that can benefit you during your time behind bars. Instead of getting caught up in gambling, consider investing your time and energy in activities that can help you grow and improve yourself.

Pursuing education, engaging in prison activities, or even maintaining employment within the prison system can be more fulfilling and beneficial in the long run. These activities not only keep you occupied but also contribute to your personal development and growth. If you find yourself tempted to participate in gambling, you should remind yourself of those potential consequences. Losing money in bets can lead to financial strain and even debt within the prison community.

Additionally, disputes over gambling debts can escalate into conflicts that put your safety at risk. It's crucial to prioritize your well-being and avoid putting yourself in compromising situations. Seek, out healthy alternatives to gambling that can help you stay focused and motivated during your time in prison. Building relationships based on trust and mutual respect, engaging in productive activities, and focusing on self-improvement can lead to a more positive and fulfilling experience behind bars.

By avoiding gambling and making wise choices, you can navigate prison life with resilience and integrity.

twelve
securing belongings

IN A PRISON ENVIRONMENT, one of the most critical aspects of surviving is securing your belongings. Your possessions hold value, both practically and emotionally, and losing them can lead to a variety of problems. Here, we will discuss the importance of safeguarding your belongings and offer tips on how to protect them within the confines of a correctional facility.

When serving time in prison, your personal items become even more precious. They may be your only connection to the outside world, reminding you of who you are beyond the prison walls. Therefore, it is essential to take measures to keep them safe and secure.

First and foremost, always keep your belongings organized and in a designated place. This not only helps you keep track of your items but also makes it easier to notice if something is missing. By maintaining a system for your possessions, you can quickly identify any discrepancies and take action before it's too late. Additionally, it is advisable to label your belongings discreetly. Marking your items with your initials or a unique symbol can help prevent confusion or intentional misplacement.

This simple step can discourage others, from claiming your personal belongings as their own and reduce the likelihood of disputes. Furthermore, when it comes to storing your valuables, opt for secure containers or designated storage areas if available. Lockers or personal lockboxes can provide an extra layer of protection for your important items, such as legal documents, letters from loved ones, or cherished personal effects.

It is also crucial to be mindful of your surroundings and the people you interact with. Building trust with fellow inmates can be beneficial, but always exercise caution when sharing information about your belongings. Avoid displaying your valuables openly or discussing their whereabouts with others, as this can attract unwanted attention and potential theft. In the event that you do discover a missing or stolen item, report it to the appropriate authorities immediately.

By taking prompt action and documenting the incident, you increase the chances of recovering your belongings and holding the responsible party accountable.

Remember, securing your belongings is not just about protecting material possessions; it is also about safeguarding your sense of security and privacy. By following these guidelines and remaining vigilant, you can minimize the risk of losing your personal items and maintain a sense of control in an environment where so much is beyond your control.

thirteen **being wary of predators**

IN AN ENVIRONMENT as volatile as a prison, it is crucial to be vigilant and cautious in your interactions with others. Predators may lurk among the inmate population, looking to take advantage of those who appear vulnerable or naive.

Being aware of potential threats and taking steps to protect yourself is essential for your safety and well-being during your time behind bars.

Navigating Inmates: When interacting with fellow inmates, it is important to be discerning and observant. Not everyone in prison has your best interests at heart, and some individuals may try to manipulate or exploit you for their own gain. Be cautious of those who seem overly friendly or eager to establish a connection too quickly.

Reciprocating Favors: While it is common for inmates to help each other out with favors or tasks, be wary of individuals who expect something in return for their assistance. Predators may use this tactic to create a sense of indebtedness and later exploit it for their benefit. Only agree to favors that you feel comfortable reciprocating without feeling pressured or obligated.

Building Trust: Trust should be earned gradually and not given lightly in a prison setting. Predators may try to gain your trust through flattery or promises of protection, only to later betray you for their own gain. Take the time to get to know individuals before confiding in them or relying on them for support.

Rejecting Control: Predators may attempt to exert control over you through intimidation or coercion. It is essential to assert your independence and autonomy in your interactions with others. Refuse to be manipulated or bullied into doing things that make you uncomfortable or compromise your values.

Protecting Personal Information: Be cautious about sharing personal details or sensitive information with other inmates, especially those you do not know well. Predators may use this information against you or exploit it to gain leverage in their interactions with you. Keep your personal matters private and only disclose information to individuals you trust.

Observing Table Etiquette: Maintaining proper etiquette at mealtimes can help you avoid unnecessary conflicts or confrontations with other inmates. Be mindful of your manners and respectful of others' space and boundaries in the dining area. Avoid engaging in behaviors that may attract unwanted attention or provoke negative reactions from fellow inmates.

By being vigilant and cautious in your interactions with others, you can protect yourself from potential predators and ensure your safety and well-being during your time in prison. Stay alert, trust your instincts, and prioritize your own security above all else.

fourteen
building trust

NAVIGATING the complex social dynamics within a prison environment requires a delicate balance of various factors. One crucial element that can significantly impact your experience behind bars is the ability to build and maintain trust.

Trust forms the foundation of relationships, alliances, and interactions with both inmates and staff. In a setting where suspicion and uncertainty loom large, establishing trust can be the key to a smoother and safer prison stay. When it comes to building trust in prison, authenticity is paramount. Being genuine in your words and actions can help others see you as a reliable and trustworthy individual.

Consistency is also crucial - following through on your promises and commitments will show others that they can depend on you. Trust is fragile, and once broken, it can be challenging to repair. Therefore, it is vital to prioritize honesty and integrity in all your interactions. Another essential aspect of building trust in prison is respecting boundaries and privacy. Everyone has their personal space and limits, and being mindful of these boundaries can earn you respect and trust from your peers.

Avoiding gossip and spreading rumors can also contribute to

building trust, as it shows that you can be discreet and trustworthy with sensitive information. In a prison environment, trust can also be built through acts of kindness and support.

Offering help to others when needed, sharing resources, and showing empathy can help foster positive relationships and build trust within the community. Reciprocity plays a significant role in establishing trust - by giving back and reciprocating favors, you demonstrate your willingness to contribute to the well-being of the group.

Moreover, demonstrating trustworthiness in your behavior can help you gain the trust of others. Following the rules, respecting authority, and maintaining a positive attitude can all contribute to building trust within the prison community. By showing that you are a reliable and responsible individual, you can earn the respect and trust of your peers.

Overall, building trust in a prison setting requires effort, consistency, and integrity. By being authentic, respectful, and supportive, you can establish positive relationships and navigate the complexities of the prison environment more effectively.

Trust is a valuable currency in prison, and investing in building and maintaining it can enhance your experience and safety during your time behind bars.

fifteen
self-defense strategies

IN THE ENVIRONMENT OF A PRISON, it is essential to be aware of various situations that may arise and to be prepared to handle them wisely. Self-defense strategies are not only about physical protection but also encompass mental and emotional defense mechanisms. By understanding how to navigate through potential conflicts and dangerous scenarios, you can better protect yourself and maintain your well-being during your time in prison.

Here, we will explore some key aspects of self-defense strategies that can help you stay safe and secure while incarcerated. Borrowing Money: One common practice in prison is borrowing money from fellow inmates. While it may seem like a quick solution to financial needs, it can lead to conflicts and potential dangers if not handled carefully. When borrowing money, make sure to clearly establish the terms of the loan, including the repayment schedule and any interest rates. Avoid borrowing more than you can reasonably repay, as this could put you in a vulnerable position. Always prioritize repaying your debts promptly to avoid any misunderstandings or confrontations.

Witnessing Violence: Violence can occur unexpectedly in a prison setting, and witnessing such incidents can be unsettling and frightening. If you find yourself in a situation where violence is unfolding, it is crucial to prioritize your safety above all else. Avoid getting directly involved in altercations unless absolutely necessary for self-defense.

Instead, seek a safe place to sit or stand away from the violence taking place and if possible, away from any other prisoners, to ensure your well-being. It is essential to stay out of it absolutely, and not report any incidents of violence that you witness to the prison authorities, to prevent harm against you by other inmates and maintain a safe environment for yourself.

Avoiding Crowds: Crowded areas in prison can be breeding grounds for tension and conflicts. To protect yourself, it is advisable to avoid large crowds whenever possible. By staying away from overcrowded spaces, you can reduce the likelihood of getting caught up in disputes or confrontations. If you must navigate through a crowded area, maintain a low profile, keep to yourself, and be mindful of your surroundings. Remember that your safety is paramount, and avoiding unnecessary risks by steering clear of crowded areas can help you stay out of harm's way.

Consequences of Snitching: Snitching, or informing on fellow inmates to authorities, can have serious repercussions in a prison setting. While it may seem like a way to gain favor or protection, the act of snitching can lead to distrust, retaliation, and even violence from other inmates. It is crucial to understand the potential consequences of snitching and weigh the risks before taking any action. Instead of resorting to snitching, focus on building positive relationships based on trust and mutual respect with your peers. By avoiding involvement in conflicts and disputes that do not concern you directly, you can protect yourself from the dangers associated with snitching.

Keeping Your Word: In a prison environment, your word and reputation carry significant weight. Honesty, integrity, and reliability are valued traits that can help you earn the respect of your fellow inmates and build trust within the community. When you make commitments or agreements with others, it is essential to honor your word and follow through on your promises. By keeping your word and demonstrating consistency in your actions, you can establish yourself as a trustworthy individual who is respected by others. Remember that maintaining your credibility and upholding your integrity are essential components of self-defense strategies that can safeguard your reputation and well-being in prison.

Navigating Inmates: Interacting with a diverse group of inmates in prison requires tact, diplomacy, and awareness of your surroundings. To navigate effectively among your peers, it is essential to be observant, respectful, and discerning in your interactions. Avoid getting involved in gossip, rumors, or divisive conversations that could lead to misunderstandings or conflicts. Instead, focus on building positive relationships based on mutual respect, empathy, and understanding.

By treating others with kindness and consideration, you can create a supportive network of allies who can help protect you and provide assistance when needed. Navigating inmates with diplomacy and tact is a crucial self-defense strategy that can help you establish a sense of belonging and security within the prison community.

sixteen
protecting legal information

IN PRISON, safeguarding your legal information is paramount to protecting your rights and ensuring fair treatment. Legal documents and conversations with your attorney are confidential and should remain so to uphold your defense. Here are key points to consider in protecting your legal information while incarcerated:

1. **Understanding Confidentiality**: Legal information is private and should only be shared with your attorney or legal representatives. Avoid discussing your case with other inmates or staff members.
2. **Secure Storage**: Keep your legal documents in a safe place, such as a locked locker or filing cabinet. Do not leave them out in the open where they can be accessed by others.
3. **Avoid Sharing Details**: Refrain from discussing the specifics of your case with fellow inmates, as this information could be used against you or jeopardize your defense.
4. **Communicate Privately**: When speaking with your attorney, ensure that your conversations are

confidential and not overheard by others. Use designated areas for legal consultations.

5. **Be Cautious with Written Correspondence**: Letters to and from your attorney should be marked as confidential and sealed properly. Avoid sharing legal details in letters to friends or family members.
6. **Report Breaches**: If you suspect that your legal information has been compromised or shared without authorization, report it to the appropriate authorities immediately.
7. **Educate Yourself**: Understand your rights regarding legal information protection within the prison system. Familiarize yourself with the procedures for accessing legal resources and maintaining confidentiality.
8. **Maintain Trust**: Build a strong relationship with your legal team based on trust and open communication. Ensure that they are aware of any concerns regarding the confidentiality of your information.
9. **Stay Informed**: Keep yourself updated on any changes in regulations or policies related to legal information protection in the prison environment. Knowledge is key to safeguarding your rights.
10. **Respect Attorney-Client Privilege**: Recognize the importance of attorney-client privilege and uphold the confidentiality of your discussions with your legal counsel. This privilege is crucial in maintaining the integrity of your defense.

By following these guidelines, you can protect your legal information and ensure that your rights are upheld during your time in prison. Safeguarding this critical information is essential for a fair and just legal process.

seventeen
respecting property

RESPECTING Property is crucial while serving time in prison. It involves understanding the boundaries and respecting the belongings of others. By following this principle, you can avoid conflicts and maintain a sense of order within the prison community. It's important to remember that personal property is a significant aspect of an inmate's life. Just as you would want your belongings to be respected, you should treat others' property with the same level of care and consideration. Here are some key points to keep in mind when it comes to respecting property:

1. **Avoid Taking What Isn't Yours**: This may seem obvious, but it's essential to never take something that belongs to another inmate without their permission. This includes food, clothing, toiletries, or any other personal items.
2. **Respect Personal Space**: Be mindful of others' living areas and avoid entering or tampering with their personal space without permission. Everyone deserves a sense of privacy, even in a shared environment like a prison.

3. **Report Damages**: If you accidentally damage someone else's property, it's important to take responsibility and report it promptly. Honesty and accountability go a long way in maintaining respect within the prison community.
4. **Follow the Rules**: Each facility will have specific guidelines regarding the use and care of property. Make sure to familiarize yourself with these rules and adhere to them diligently to avoid any misunderstandings or conflicts.
5. **Help Maintain Order**: showing respect for property, you contribute to a sense of order and mutual respect among inmates. This can help create a safer and more harmonious environment for everyone.
6. **Lead by Example**: Show others the importance of respecting property through your actions. Demonstrating a high level of respect for others' belongings, you set a positive example for those around you. In conclusion, respecting property is not just about following rules; it's a reflection of your character and values.

By treating others' belongings with care and consideration, you contribute to a culture of respect and mutual understanding within the prison community. Remember, how you treat others' property speaks volumes about your integrity and respect for others.

eighteen
dealing with theft

IN A PRISON SETTING, theft can unfortunately be a common occurrence. It's important to understand how to navigate this issue to protect yourself and your belongings. Here are some key points to keep in mind when dealing with theft while serving time:

1. **Securing Your Belongings**: One of the best ways to prevent theft is by ensuring your belongings are secure at all times. Keep your personal items in a locked locker or storage unit when not in use.
2. **Being Wary of Predators**: Some inmates may try to take advantage of others by stealing from them. Be cautious of individuals who exhibit predatory behavior and try to avoid associating with them.
3. **Building Trust**: Establishing trustworthy relationships with fellow inmates can help reduce the likelihood of theft. Surround yourself with people you can rely on and who have your back.
4. **Protecting Personal Information**: Avoid sharing sensitive information about your possessions or

finances with others. Keep personal details private to prevent potential theft.

5. **Dealing with Theft**: If you become a victim of theft, it's essential to report the incident to prison authorities. They can investigate the matter and take appropriate actions to address the situation.
6. **Maintaining Silence**: While it may be tempting to retaliate or confront the thief yourself, it's crucial to avoid engaging in any violence or illegal activities. Let the authorities handle the situation.
7. **Respecting Property**: Treat others' belongings with respect to set a positive example and reduce the risk of retaliation or conflict.
8. **Engaging in Prison Activities**: Keeping yourself occupied with constructive activities can help distract you from potential theft incidents. Participating in programs and classes can also help you build positive relationships with others.
9. **Navigating Inmates**: Be aware of who's around you, observant of your surroundings, and the people you interact with. Trust your instincts and avoid individuals who exhibit suspicious behavior.
10. **Protecting Legal Information**: Keep your legal documents and information safe and confidential. This can prevent theft of sensitive materials that could impact your case or legal standing.

By following these guidelines and staying vigilant, you can better protect yourself and your belongings from theft while serving time in prison. Remember, it's crucial to prioritize your safety and well-being in any situation.

nineteen
engaging in prison activities

ENGAGING in Prison Activities Prison life can be challenging, but there are ways to stay engaged and make the most of your time behind bars. Engaging in prison activities is not only a way to pass the time but also an opportunity to learn, grow, and connect with others in a positive manner.

Here are some tips on how to stay active and involved in various activities while serving your time.

1. **Participate in Educational Programs**: Many prisons offer educational programs that can help you expand your knowledge and skills. Whether it's earning a GED or taking vocational courses, engaging in these activities can not only pass the time but also set you up for success upon release.
2. **Join a Book Club**: Reading can be a great way to escape the reality of prison life. Consider joining a book club where you can discuss literature with other inmates and broaden your perspectives.
3. **Attend Religious Services**: If you are religious, attending religious services can provide you with a

sense of community and spiritual support during your time in prison.

4. **Volunteer for Work Assignments**: Keeping busy with work assignments can help you stay productive and focused. Whether it's working in the kitchen, laundry room, or library, volunteering for these tasks can give you a sense of purpose.
5. **Exercise Regularly**: Physical activity is not only good for your physical health but can also improve your mental well-being. Engage in regular exercise routines or join sports activities to stay active and release stress.
6. **Learn a New Skill**: Use your time in prison to learn a new skill or hobby. Whether it's painting, playing a musical instrument, or even writing, exploring new interests can be fulfilling and enriching.
7. **Participate in Support Groups**: Joining support groups can provide you with a safe space to share your thoughts and feelings with others who may be going through similar experiences.
8. **Engage in Art Therapy**: Art therapy can be a therapeutic way to express yourself and process your emotions. Consider participating in art classes or workshops to tap into your creative side.
9. **Write in a Journal**: Keeping a journal can be a cathartic way to document your thoughts, reflections, and experiences while in prison. It can also serve as a form of self-expression and self-discovery.
10. **Start a Study Group**: Collaborating with fellow inmates to study together can help you stay motivated and accountable in your educational pursuits.

By engaging in these various prison activities, you can make the most of your time behind bars and work towards personal growth and development. Stay proactive, stay engaged, and stay positive as you navigate through your prison sentence.

twenty
managing stress

DEALING with stress while serving time in prison can be one of the biggest challenges inmates face. The environment is inherently tense, and the lack of freedom can take a toll on mental well-being. However, there are strategies you can employ to manage stress and maintain your mental health during your time behind bars.

First and foremost, it's essential to find healthy coping mechanisms. Engaging in physical exercise, meditation, or art can help channel your emotions in a positive way. These activities can provide a much-needed break from the everyday pressures of prison life and help you relax and refocus.

Another crucial aspect of managing stress is seeking support from others. Building a network of trustworthy individuals can provide a sense of camaraderie and understanding. Talking to someone you trust about your worries and fears can lighten the emotional burden and offer a fresh perspective on your situation. It's also important to set realistic expectations for yourself.

Understand that you are in a challenging environment, and it's okay to feel overwhelmed at times. Allow yourself to experience your emotions without judgment and seek help if you find yourself struggling to cope. Furthermore, maintaining a routine can help create a sense of stability and control in an otherwise unpredictable environment.

Establishing a daily schedule that includes time for relaxation, exercise, and social interactions can help you stay grounded and focused on your well-being. Avoiding negative influences and toxic relationships is crucial for managing stress. Surround yourself with positive and supportive individuals who uplift and encourage you. Steer clear of drama and conflict that can exacerbate your stress levels and impact your mental health.

Lastly, remember to prioritize self-care. Take care of your physical health by eating well, getting enough sleep, and practicing good hygiene. Your body and mind are interconnected, and taking care of one will positively impact the other.

By incorporating these strategies into your daily life, you can effectively manage stress and maintain your mental well-being while serving time in prison. Remember that your mental health is just as important as your physical health, and taking proactive steps to address stress can lead to a more positive and fulfilling experience during your incarceration.

twenty-one
maintaining hygiene

MAINTAINING Hygiene is essential for not only your health but also your overall well-being while serving time in prison. In a confined space with many individuals, it's crucial to practice good hygiene habits to prevent the spread of germs and diseases. Here are some important tips to help you maintain hygiene in prison:

1. **Shower Regularly**: Make it a habit to shower daily if possible. Proper hygiene starts with keeping your body clean.
2. **Wash Your Hands**: Always wash your hands before and after meals, after using the restroom, and whenever necessary. Hand-washing is one of the most effective ways to prevent infections.
3. **Brush Your Teeth**: Dental hygiene is important. Brush your teeth at least twice a day and don't forget to floss.
4. **Keep Your Living Area Clean**: Take the time to tidy up your living space regularly. A clean environment is conducive to good hygiene.
5. **Wear Clean Clothes**: Change into clean clothes

regularly and wash them when needed. Dirty clothing can harbor bacteria and odors.

6. **Trim Nails**: Keep your nails short and clean to prevent the buildup of dirt and bacteria.
7. **Properly Dispose of Waste**: Use designated trash cans and disposal methods for any waste to maintain cleanliness.
8. **Avoid Sharing Personal Items**: Sharing personal items like towels, razors, or clothing can spread germs. Stick to using your own belongings.
9. **Report Any Hygiene Issues**: If you notice any hygiene problems in shared facilities, report them to the appropriate authorities for resolution.
10. **Use Personal Hygiene Products**: Make sure to have your own soap, shampoo, toothpaste, and other personal hygiene products to maintain cleanliness.
11. **Don't Neglect Your Feet**: Keep your feet clean and dry to prevent fungal infections like athlete's foot.
12. **Practice Good Toilet Hygiene**: Always flush after use, clean up after yourself, and follow proper toilet etiquette to prevent the spread of germs.

By following these hygiene practices, you can contribute to a cleaner and healthier environment for yourself and those around you. Remember, maintaining hygiene is not just about appearances; it's about safeguarding your health and well-being in a challenging environment like prison.

twenty-two
utilizing the law library

INCARCERATION CAN BE a challenging and complex experience, but there are ways to navigate through it with knowledge and awareness. One valuable resource available to inmates is the law library. Understanding how to utilize the law library effectively can make a significant difference in your time served.

Here are some key points to keep in mind when it comes to making the most of the law library:

1. **Understanding Legal Resources**: The law library is a treasure trove of legal information that can help you navigate the criminal justice system. Familiarize yourself with the resources available, such as legal books, journals, and online databases.
2. **Seeking Legal Assistance**: If you have a legal issue or need advice on your case, the law library can be a valuable resource. Look for legal aid materials or ask the library staff for guidance on how to access legal assistance.
3. **Researching Your Case**: Use the law library to research legal precedents, case law, and statutes relevant to your situation. This can help you better

understand your rights and options within the legal system.

4. **Preparing Legal Documents**: The law library may have templates and guides to help you draft legal documents such as appeals, petitions, or motions. Take advantage of these resources to ensure your paperwork is accurate and well-prepared.
5. **Staying Informed**: Keep up to date with changes in the law that may affect your case or rights. Regularly check legal publications and resources in the law library to stay informed about legal developments.
6. **Respecting the Space**: The law library is a place for serious study and research. Respect the quiet atmosphere and the needs of other inmates who are using the resources. Keep noise to a minimum and maintain a respectful attitude towards the staff and fellow users.
7. **Following Rules and Guidelines**: Each law library may have specific rules and guidelines for its use. Make sure to familiarize yourself with these rules and adhere to them to avoid any disruptions or conflicts.
8. **Seeking Help When Needed**: If you are unsure about how to use a legal resource or need assistance with your research, don't hesitate to ask the library staff for help. They are there to support you in your legal endeavors.

By utilizing the law library effectively, you can empower yourself with knowledge, improve your legal understanding, and potentially make a positive impact on your case. Take advantage of this valuable resource to navigate the legal complexities of incarceration with confidence and awareness.

twenty-three
pursuing education

IN THE COMPLEX and challenging environment of prison, pursuing education can be a valuable tool for personal growth and development. While serving time behind bars, engaging in educational activities can provide a sense of purpose, stimulate the mind, and offer a path towards self-improvement.

Here are some key points to consider when it comes to pursuing education while incarcerated:

Utilize Available Resources: Prisons often offer educational programs, such as GED courses, vocational training, or even college classes. Take advantage of these opportunities to further your knowledge and skills.

Set Goals: Determine what you want to achieve through education while in prison. Whether it's earning a degree, learning a new trade, or simply expanding your horizons, having clear goals can help you stay focused and motivated.

Develop a Study Routine: Establish a regular study schedule to dedicate time to your educational pursuits. Consistency is key in making progress and maximizing your learning potential.

Seek Mentorship: If possible, connect with fellow inmates who are knowledgeable in the subjects you're interested in or have experience with the educational programs available. Learning from others can provide valuable insights and support.

Stay Disciplined: Education in prison requires commitment and discipline. Stay dedicated to your studies, even when faced with distractions or setbacks. Remember that the effort you put in now can have a positive impact on your future.

Stay Positive: Education is a powerful tool for personal transformation and growth. Maintain a positive attitude towards learning, even when faced with challenges or obstacles. Embrace the opportunity to expand your knowledge and skills.

Apply What You Learn: Take the knowledge and skills you acquire through education and apply them to real-life situations. Whether it's in your personal development, interactions with others, or future career opportunities, education can empower you to make positive changes in your life.

Share Your Knowledge: As you progress in your educational journey, consider sharing what you've learned with others. Teaching or tutoring fellow inmates can not only reinforce your own understanding but also contribute to a supportive learning community within the prison environment.

By actively pursuing education while in prison, you can transform your time behind bars into a period of personal growth, learning, and self-improvement. Education has the power to open doors, broaden perspectives, and empower you to build a better future for yourself. Embrace the opportunity to learn, grow, and thrive, even in the midst of challenging circumstances.

twenty-four
running an inmate store

RUNNING a store in prison can be a valuable way to earn some extra income, establish relationships with fellow inmates, and provide access to goods that may not be readily available otherwise. However, it also comes with its own set of challenges and considerations that must be carefully navigated to ensure success and safety within the prison environment.

When running a store in prison, it is essential to establish a clear system for inventory management, sales, and customer service.

Keep detailed records of your stock, sales, and profits to track your business performance and prevent any discrepancies or disputes among customers.

Maintain a consistent pricing strategy to ensure fairness and avoid conflicts with customers.

Clearly communicate your prices and any special promotions to avoid misunderstandings or accusations of price gouging. Build trust with your customers by providing quality products, reliable services, and fair dealings.

Honesty and integrity are crucial in developing a loyal customer base and fostering positive relationships within the prison community. Be mindful of the potential risks associated with running a store in prison, such as theft, extortion, or conflicts with other inmates.

Take necessary precautions to secure your inventory, finances, and personal safety. Avoid carrying large sums of money or valuable items that may make you a target for theft or violence.

Establish clear boundaries with customers and vendors to maintain a professional and respectful business environment. Set expectations for behavior, transactions, and disputes resolution to prevent misunderstandings and conflicts from escalating.

Collaborate with other inmates or trusted individuals to help manage your store operations, share responsibilities, and expand your business offerings. Building a network of reliable partners can enhance the efficiency and profitability of your store while reducing the burden of running it single-handedly.

Stay informed about the rules and regulations governing store operations in prison to avoid any violations or sanctions that could jeopardize your business. Seek guidance from experienced inmates or prison staff on compliance requirements and best practices for running a store within the facility.

Overall, running a store in prison can be a rewarding and challenging experience that requires careful planning, dedication, and resilience.

By following these guidelines and maintaining a proactive approach to managing your store, you can navigate the complexities of prison entrepreneurship successfully and contribute positively to your inmate community.

twenty-five
practicing respect

RESPECTING others is a fundamental aspect of navigating life in prison. In this environment, where tensions can run high and conflicts easily arise, showing respect can go a long way in maintaining relationships and ensuring your own safety.

When interacting with fellow inmates, it's important to treat them with dignity and consideration. This means refraining from belittling or insulting language, avoiding confrontations, and being mindful of personal boundaries.

By showing respect, you can help defuse potentially volatile situations and foster a more positive atmosphere within the prison community. Respect also extends to property and belongings. Whether it's shared facilities or personal items, being mindful of others' possessions and treating them with care demonstrates your consideration for those around you.

Refrain from taking what isn't yours and always ask for permission before using someone else's belongings. Furthermore, respecting conversations and privacy is crucial. Avoid eavesdropping on others' discussions, and refrain from sharing personal information that isn't yours to disclose. Protecting the confidentiality of others demonstrates your trustworthiness and integrity, qualities that are valued in a prison setting.

When it comes to guard relationships, maintaining a respectful demeanor is essential. While it's natural to have frustrations and grievances, expressing them in a respectful and constructive manner can help address issues more effectively. Avoiding conflicts with guards and following their instructions can contribute to a smoother and more peaceful environment for everyone.

In conclusion, practicing respect in all aspects of prison life is not only beneficial for your own well-being but also contributes to a more harmonious and secure environment for all. By treating others with consideration, valuing their property and privacy, and maintaining respectful interactions, you can navigate the challenges of prison life with dignity and integrity.

twenty-six
rejecting control

IN A PRISON ENVIRONMENT, maintaining a sense of autonomy and self-determination can be challenging. The power dynamics at play can often lead to individuals feeling as though they have little control over their own lives. However, it is crucial to remember that even in such circumstances, there are ways to assert your independence and reject unnecessary control from others.

One of the key strategies for rejecting control is to set clear boundaries with those around you. Whether it be other inmates, guards, or even prison staff, it is important to communicate your limits and expectations clearly. By doing so, you can establish a sense of agency and control over your own actions and decisions. Another important aspect of rejecting control is to avoid becoming overly reliant on others for validation or support.

While it may be tempting to seek approval from fellow inmates or authority figures, it is essential to remember that true empowerment comes from within. By cultivating a strong sense of self-worth and self-reliance, you can resist the influence of those who seek to control or manipulate you. Additionally, it is vital to advocate for yourself and your rights within the prison system. This may involve speaking up against injustices, reporting abuse or misconduct, and seeking legal assistance when necessary. By asserting yourself in a respectful and assertive manner, you can demonstrate that you will not be easily controlled or silenced.

Furthermore, developing a strong support network of trusted individuals can help you navigate the complexities of prison life while maintaining your sense of independence.

By surrounding yourself with people who respect your boundaries and support your autonomy, you can create a positive and empowering environment for yourself. Ultimately, rejecting control in a prison setting requires a combination of assertiveness, self-reliance, and advocacy.

By setting boundaries, valuing yourself, advocating for your rights, and building a supportive network, you can assert your independence and resist undue influence from others. Remember, you have the power to shape your own destiny, even in the most challenging of circumstances.

twenty-seven
maintaining employment

AS YOU NAVIGATE your time in prison, it's essential to consider how you can maintain employment even within the confines of the correctional facility. While serving your sentence, it's crucial to find ways to stay productive and possibly earn some income.

Here are some tips to help you in this endeavor:

1. **Utilize Your Skills**: Assess your abilities and see if there are any work opportunities within the prison that align with your expertise. Whether it's cleaning, cooking, or maintenance work, find a role that suits your skills.
2. **Stay Professional**: Treat any job within the prison with professionalism. Show up on time, complete your tasks diligently, and maintain a positive attitude towards your work responsibilities.
3. **Seek Opportunities**: Keep an eye out for job openings or tasks that need to be done. By being proactive and willing to take on various roles, you can increase your chances of securing employment.

4. **Build Relationships**: Establish good relationships with the staff members who oversee work assignments. By demonstrating your reliability and work ethic, you may be considered for more job opportunities.
5. **Show Initiative**: Don't wait for work to come to you. If you notice areas that need attention or improvement, take the initiative to address them. This proactive approach can showcase your commitment to work.
6. **Learn New Skills**: Use your time in prison to acquire new skills or enhance existing ones. Whether through vocational training programs or self-study, expanding your skill set can make you more employable within the facility.
7. **Network**: Build connections with other inmates who are employed or involved in work programs. Networking can open up new job opportunities and provide support in your employment endeavors.
8. **Follow Rules**: Adhere to all regulations and guidelines related to employment within the prison. By following the rules, you demonstrate your respect for authority and your willingness to work within the system.
9. **Stay Committed**: Consistency is key when it comes to maintaining employment. Show dedication to your work responsibilities and strive to excel in whatever tasks you are assigned.
10. **Seek Feedback**: Don't be afraid to ask for feedback on your performance. Constructive criticism can help you improve and grow in your role, making you a more valuable employee.

By actively seeking out employment opportunities, demonstrating professionalism, and continually improving your skills, you can maintain employment while serving your time in prison.

Remember that staying engaged in work can not only provide a sense of purpose but also contribute to your personal growth and development during your incarceration.

twenty-eight
protecting privacy

PROTECTING Privacy In the challenging environment of prison, privacy is a precious commodity that must be safeguarded at all costs. Your personal information, thoughts, and actions should be shielded from unwanted eyes and ears to maintain a sense of control and security in an otherwise restrictive setting.

Here are some essential tips to help you protect your privacy while serving time.

1. **Guarding Personal Information** One of the first steps in preserving your privacy in prison is to guard your personal information zealously. Avoid sharing details about your past, family, or criminal history with fellow inmates unless absolutely necessary. Protecting your identity can prevent others from manipulating or exploiting you based on this knowledge.
2. **Securing Communication** When communicating with loved ones or legal counsel, ensure that your conversations are private and cannot be overheard. Use designated phone areas or visitation rooms where confidentiality is better maintained. Be cautious of

discussions that could compromise your case or put you at risk within the prison community.

3. **Protecting Written Correspondence** Written correspondence, such as letters or notes, can be a vulnerable point for privacy breaches. Seal your envelopes securely, avoid sharing sensitive information in writing, and consider using coded language if necessary. Be mindful of where you store your letters to prevent unauthorized access.
4. **Maintaining Boundaries** Establish clear boundaries with fellow inmates and staff regarding your personal space and possessions. Respect others' privacy in return, but also assert your right to privacy when needed. Avoid sharing intimate details or engaging in gossip that could compromise your relationships or reputation.
5. **Avoiding Idle Gossip** Rumors and gossip can spread quickly in a confined environment like prison, leading to potential privacy violations. Refrain from sharing personal details or engaging in conversations that could attract unwanted attention or scrutiny. Focus on building meaningful relationships based on trust and respect.
6. **Using Discretion** Practice discretion in your interactions and activities to prevent unnecessary exposure of your private affairs. Avoid drawing attention to yourself through excessive boasting, confrontations, or risky behaviors that could invite unwanted scrutiny. Cultivate a reputation for being discreet and trustworthy.
7. **Keeping a Low Profile** While it's essential to maintain social connections in prison, keeping a low profile can also protect your privacy. Avoid drawing unnecessary attention to yourself through flashy possessions or disruptive behavior. Blend in with the

crowd while maintaining your individuality in a subtle manner.

8. **Seeking Confidential Support** If you encounter privacy breaches or feel your boundaries are being violated, seek confidential support from trusted individuals or prison staff. Report any instances of harassment, intimidation, or invasion of privacy to the appropriate authorities to address the issue promptly.

By implementing these strategies and staying vigilant about protecting your privacy, you can navigate the complexities of prison life with greater confidence and security. Your personal information and boundaries are valuable assets that deserve to be respected, even in the most challenging circumstances.

twenty-nine
avoiding conflict

IN THE COMPLEX and challenging environment of prison, navigating through various situations while avoiding conflict is crucial for your safety and well-being. Let's delve into the 40 do's and don'ts that can help you steer clear of trouble and maintain a sense of peace during your time behind bars.

Borrowing Money: It may be tempting to borrow money from fellow inmates, but be cautious. Debts can quickly escalate, leading to conflicts and potential violence. It's best to live within your means and avoid getting entangled in financial obligations that could put you at risk.

Witnessing Violence: If you witness violence in prison, it's essential to report it discreetly to the authorities. However, avoid getting directly involved in altercations as it could escalate and jeopardize your safety. Your priority should be to stay safe and seek help when needed.

Avoiding Crowds: In crowded areas of the prison, tensions can run high, increasing the likelihood of conflicts. Try to navigate your way through crowded spaces calmly and avoid confrontation by keeping to yourself whenever possible. Remember, staying out of the crowd can often mean staying out of trouble.

Consequences of Snitching: While it is lawful to report illegal activities to the authorities, being labeled as a snitch in prison can have severe consequences. To avoid conflict, tread carefully when sharing information and consider the potential risks before deciding to report any misconduct.

Keeping Your Word: In a place where trust is scarce, keeping your word is essential. Be reliable and true to your commitments to build trust with your fellow inmates. Breaking promises or agreements can lead to conflicts and damage your reputation within the prison community.

Navigating Inmates: Interacting with a diverse range of inmates requires tact and diplomacy. Treat others with respect, avoid gossip or spreading rumors, and be mindful of cultural and social differences. By navigating inmate relationships thoughtfully, you can minimize conflicts and foster positive connections.

Reciprocating Favors: In prison, favors are often exchanged as a form of social currency. If someone does you a favor, try to reciprocate when possible. Failing to do so could strain relationships and lead to conflicts. Remember, kindness and gratitude go a long way in maintaining harmony.

Drugs and Tattoos: Engaging in drug use or getting tattoos in prison can have serious consequences, including conflicts with other inmates or disciplinary actions. Stay clear of these activities to protect yourself and avoid unnecessary trouble. Focus on staying clean and safe during your time in prison.

Interacting with Others: Effective communication is key to avoiding conflicts in prison. Be clear, assertive, and respectful when interacting with others. Listen actively, choose your words wisely, and avoid misunderstandings that could escalate into confrontations.

Maintaining Silence: Sometimes, silence is your best ally in avoiding conflicts. If you find yourself in a tense situation or facing aggression, staying calm and composed can help defuse the tension. Choose your battles wisely and know when to remain silent to protect yourself.

Avoiding Gambling: Gambling in prison can lead to debt, disputes, and even violence. Avoid getting involved in gambling activities to steer clear of unnecessary conflicts and safeguard your well-being. Focus on productive and safe ways to pass the time instead. Securing Belongings: Protect your personal belongings in prison by keeping them secure and out of sight. Theft can spark conflicts and disrupt your peace of mind. Utilize lockers or designated storage areas to safeguard your possessions and avoid unnecessary confrontations.

Being Wary of Predators: Stay vigilant and cautious of individuals who may try to take advantage of you or manipulate you in prison. Predators often prey on vulnerable individuals, so trust your instincts and seek support from trusted allies to avoid falling victim to their schemes. Building Trust: Trust is a valuable commodity in prison and can help you navigate relationships and conflicts effectively. Be honest, reliable, and true to your word to build trust with others. By fostering genuine connections based on trust, you can reduce the likelihood of misunderstandings and disputes.

Self-Defense Strategies: While physical altercations should always be avoided, knowing basic self-defense strategies can help you protect yourself in dangerous situations. Focus on de-escalation techniques, avoiding confrontations, and seeking help from other inmates when needed. Your safety should always be your top priority.

Protecting Legal Information: Guard your legal information carefully to prevent conflicts and maintain control over your legal matters. Keep your documents secure, avoid sharing sensitive information with others, and seek legal advice from trusted sources when needed. Protecting your legal rights can help you navigate the prison system more effectively.

Respecting Property: Respect the property of others in prison to avoid conflicts and foster a sense of mutual respect. Treat shared spaces, belongings, and facilities with care and consideration. By showing respect for property, you can contribute to a more harmonious environment within the prison community.

Dealing with Theft: If you experience theft in prison, DO NOT go report it to the authorities (it will be considered snitching by other inmates); and avoid taking matters into your own hands. Retaliating against a thief can lead to conflicts and escalate the situation. Focus on protecting your belongings and seeking assistance from inmates who you trust and have favor with, within the prison community. Engaging in Prison Activities: Participating in constructive prison activities can help you stay busy, connected, and focused on positive pursuits.

Engage in educational programs, vocational training, or recreational activities to avoid conflicts and build a sense of purpose during your time in prison.

Managing Stress: Prison life can be stressful, but finding healthy ways to manage stress is essential for your well-being. Practice relaxation techniques, exercise regularly, seek support from peers or medical staff.

thirty
intercepting conversations

IN THE COMPLEX social dynamics of a prison environment, conversations play a crucial role in establishing relationships, gathering information, and maintaining connections. It is essential to navigate these interactions with caution and awareness to protect yourself and others.

Here are some key points to consider when engaging in conversations while serving time in prison:

1. **Active Listening:** When engaging in conversations, practice active listening by giving your full attention to the speaker. This shows respect and fosters better communication.
2. **Choose Your Words Wisely:** Be mindful of your language and tone during conversations. Avoid using derogatory or inflammatory language that could escalate tensions.
3. **Avoid Gossip:** Refrain from participating in gossip or spreading rumors. Engaging in gossip can damage relationships and lead to unnecessary conflicts.
4. **Maintain Confidentiality:** Respect the privacy of others by not sharing personal information without

permission. Protecting personal information builds trust and demonstrates integrity.

5. **Be Mindful of Your Surroundings:** Be aware of your surroundings when engaging in conversations. Avoid discussing sensitive or confidential matters in public areas where conversations can be overheard.
6. **Respect Boundaries:** Respect the boundaries of others during conversations. If someone is not comfortable discussing a certain topic, avoid pushing the conversation in that direction.
7. **Seek Permission:** Before sharing personal stories or information, seek permission from the other party. Respecting boundaries and privacy is crucial in maintaining healthy relationships.
8. **Clarify Misunderstandings:** If there is a misunderstanding during a conversation, address it calmly and respectfully. Clarifying misunderstandings can prevent conflicts from escalating.
9. **Stay Neutral:** Avoid taking sides or getting involved in conflicts between other inmates during conversations. Staying neutral can help prevent unnecessary confrontations.
10. **Avoid Provocation:** Refrain from provoking or instigating arguments during conversations. Maintaining a calm and respectful demeanor can help de-escalate tense situations.

Navigating conversations in a prison setting requires a delicate balance of communication skills, respect for others, and awareness of potential risks. By following these guidelines, you can protect yourself and foster positive relationships with fellow inmates.

Remember, effective communication is key to navigating the complexities of prison life and maintaining your safety and well-being.

thirty-one
avoiding guard conflict

NAVIGATING Guard Relationships In a prison setting, your interactions with guards are crucial. While it is essential to follow the rules and regulations, it is equally important to navigate these relationships with care and caution.

Here are some tips to help you avoid conflicts with prison guards and maintain a respectful and harmonious environment.

1. **Respect Their Authority:** Guards are there to enforce the rules and ensure the safety and security of the facility. It is important to show them respect and follow their instructions promptly and without resistance.
2. **Avoid Confrontations:** If you have an issue or concern, try to address it calmly and respectfully. Avoid escalating situations unnecessarily, as this could lead to conflicts with the guards.
3. **Follow Procedures:** Be familiar with the prison's procedures and regulations. By following these guidelines, you can prevent misunderstandings and conflicts with the guards.

4. **Be Courteous:** Treat guards with politeness and respect. A simple "please" and "thank you" can go a long way in fostering positive relationships with the staff.
5. **Communicate Effectively:** If you need to communicate with a guard, do so in a clear and concise manner. Avoid being confrontational or aggressive in your interactions.
6. **Report Issues Properly:** If you encounter any problems or concerns with a guard, report them through the appropriate channels. Avoid taking matters into your own hands, as this could lead to unnecessary conflicts.
7. **Avoid Manipulation:** Do not try to manipulate or deceive guards for personal gain. Honesty and integrity are essential in building trust and maintaining positive relationships.
8. **Show Appreciation:** Acknowledge the hard work and dedication of the guards. A simple gesture of gratitude can help foster positive relationships and mutual respect.
9. **Stay Informed:** Be aware of any changes in policies or procedures that may affect your interactions with guards. Staying informed can help you navigate these relationships more effectively.
10. **Remain Professional:** Remember that guards are doing their job and enforcing the rules set in place. Approach interactions with professionalism and maturity to avoid conflicts.

By following these guidelines and approaching guard relationships with respect and understanding, you can reduce the likelihood of conflicts and create a more positive environment for yourself and others in the prison setting.

thirty-two

protecting personal information

PROTECTING PERSONAL INFORMATION In a prison environment, protecting personal information is crucial for your safety and well-being. Whether it's your legal details, family contacts, or other sensitive data, keeping this information secure can help you avoid potential risks and maintain control over your own narrative.

Here are some key strategies to safeguard your personal information while serving time:

1. **Borrowing Money** When it comes to financial matters, be cautious about borrowing money from other inmates. Sharing your personal banking details or debt information can make you vulnerable to manipulation or exploitation. Only engage in financial transactions with trusted individuals, and keep your personal financial information private.
2. **Witnessing Violence** If you witness violence or illegal activities, it's essential to protect your personal information by not getting involved unnecessarily.
   - Reporting incidents to the authorities with or without revealing your identity can lead to you

being labeled a 'snitch or a rat' and becoming a target for retribution from other inmates. Your safety should always come first.

3. **Avoiding Crowds** In crowded areas, be mindful of your surroundings and avoid disclosing personal details or engaging in confidential conversations. Crowded spaces can be breeding grounds for rumors and leaks of sensitive information. Stay vigilant and protect your personal privacy.
4. **Consequences of Snitching** While it is lawful to report unlawful behavior, it is dangerous and often deadly to do so in prison. Be aware of the potential consequences of snitching. Sharing information about witnessing violence or illegal activities by other inmates, with the prison authorities, can lead to you being severely injured or even killed for doing so.
   - Consider the risks before disclosing sensitive details and weigh the potential outcomes carefully.
5. **Keeping Your Word** Maintaining your integrity and keeping your word can help build trust with fellow inmates. By honoring your commitments and staying true to your promises, you can establish a reputation as a reliable individual. This positive image can also help protect your personal information within the prison community.
6. **Navigating Inmates** Interacting with a diverse range of inmates requires caution and discretion.
   - Be selective about the personal information you share with others and avoid divulging sensitive details to individuals you don't fully trust. Navigating inmate relationships with care can safeguard your privacy.
7. **Reciprocating Favors** While it's common to exchange favors in a prison setting, be cautious about

the information you provide in return. Avoid revealing personal details or compromising information in exchange for favors. Protect your privacy by maintaining boundaries in your interactions.

8. **Drugs and Tattoos** In discussions involving drugs or tattoos, be cautious about revealing personal information that could be used against you. Avoid disclosing past drug use or gang affiliations that may compromise your safety. Protect your personal information by steering clear of conversations that could jeopardize your well-being.
9. **Interacting with Others** When interacting with other inmates, be mindful of the personal information you share. Limit discussions about your family, legal matters, or financial situation to trusted individuals. Protecting your personal details in conversations can help prevent exploitation or manipulation.
10. **Maintaining Silence** In situations where personal information is being discussed or shared, it's essential to know when to maintain silence.
    - Refrain from divulging sensitive details or engaging in conversations that could compromise your privacy. Practicing discretion and restraint can help safeguard your personal information.
11. **Avoiding Gambling** Participating in gambling activities can expose you to financial risks and potential conflicts. Avoid disclosing personal financial information or engaging in high-stakes bets that could compromise your security. Protect your personal details by steering clear of gambling activities in prison.
12. **Securing Belongings** Keep your personal belongings secure to prevent unauthorized access to your

personal information. Store important documents, letters, and personal items in a safe place and avoid leaving them unattended. Maintaining control over your belongings can help protect your privacy.

13. **Being Wary of Predators** In prison, be cautious of individuals who may try to exploit or manipulate you for personal gain. Stay vigilant and trust your instincts when interacting with others. Avoid sharing personal information with potential predators and prioritize your safety at all times.
14. **Building Trust** Establishing trust with fellow inmates can create a sense of security and camaraderie within the prison community.
    - By demonstrating honesty and reliability in your interactions, you can protect your personal information and foster positive relationships with others. Building trust can also enhance your safety and well-being.
15. **Self-Defense Strategies** While protecting your personal information is paramount, it's also essential to prioritize your physical safety. Learn self-defense strategies to defend yourself in threatening situations and safeguard your well-being. By being prepared to protect yourself, you can reduce the risk of harm and maintain control over your personal information.
16. **Protecting Legal Information** Maintaining the confidentiality of your legal information is crucial for your defense and privacy. Avoid discussing case details or legal strategies with other inmates to prevent potential breaches of confidentiality. Protecting your legal information can help you navigate the legal system effectively and safeguard your rights.
17. **Respecting Property** Respecting the property of others is essential for maintaining positive relationships and protecting your personal

information. Avoid trespassing or tampering with personal belongings, as this can lead to conflicts and breaches of privacy. By showing respect for property, you can uphold your reputation and safeguard your personal information.

18. **Dealing with Theft** If you experience theft or unauthorized access to your personal belongings, report the incident to the authorities promptly. Protecting your personal information includes taking action against theft and ensuring that your possessions are secure. Addressing theft effectively can help prevent future security breaches and safeguard your privacy.
19. **Engaging in Prison Activities** Participating in constructive prison activities can help you establish a positive reputation and protect your personal information.

thirty-three
phone etiquette

IN THE WORLD OF PRISON, communication is vital. The phone is one of the few connections to the outside world that inmates have. Therefore, it's crucial to understand the do's and don'ts of phone etiquette while serving time. When using the phone in prison, it's essential to remember that there are often limited opportunities to make calls. Be mindful of the time you spend on the phone, as others may be waiting to make important calls as well.

Always keep your conversations brief and to the point. Respect the rules and regulations surrounding phone usage.

Follow the designated schedule for phone calls and be aware of any restrictions that may be in place. Failure to adhere to these guidelines can result in consequences that could further restrict your phone privileges.

Maintain confidentiality during phone conversations. Avoid discussing sensitive information or illegal activities over the phone, as calls may be monitored or recorded. Protect your privacy and the privacy of others by being cautious about the topics you discuss. Be courteous to others when using the phone. Keep your voice down and avoid yelling or causing disruptions to those around you. Respect the space and boundaries of your fellow inmates who may also be using the phone.

Avoid using the phone for illicit activities such as coordinating criminal behavior or engaging in illegal transactions.

Remember that all phone calls are subject to monitoring and can be used as evidence against you in legal proceedings. If you receive a phone call, handle it with professionalism and discretion. Avoid sharing personal information or details about your case with unknown callers.

Be cautious of individuals who may try to manipulate you or gather information for malicious purposes.

Lastly, practice good phone etiquette by being mindful of the impact your conversations may have on others. Use the phone as a tool for staying connected with loved ones and maintaining positive relationships during your time in prison.

By following these guidelines for phone etiquette, you can navigate the complexities of communication in a correctional facility while upholding respect, privacy, and responsibility.

thirty-four
handling threats

IN THE CHALLENGING environment of prison, one must navigate various threats that can jeopardize safety and well-being. It is essential to understand how to handle these potential dangers effectively to ensure a smoother experience during incarceration. By being aware of the risks and adopting appropriate strategies, inmates can protect themselves and minimize the likelihood of harm. Let's explore some key insights on managing threats while serving time in prison.

Threats can manifest in different forms within the prison setting, ranging from physical altercations to verbal intimidation. It is crucial to remain vigilant and observant of your surroundings to identify potential threats early on. Avoiding confrontations and maintaining a low profile can help reduce the risk of becoming a target for aggression. When faced with a threatening situation, it is important to stay calm and composed. Reacting impulsively or aggressively can escalate the conflict and lead to further consequences.

Instead, consider seeking assistance from trusted individuals or prison staff to address the issue in a safe and controlled manner. Building alliances with other inmates who share similar values and principles can provide a sense of security and support. By fostering positive relationships based on mutual respect and trust, you can create a network of allies who can offer protection and guidance in times of need.

Additionally, developing effective communication skills can help diffuse potentially volatile situations. Expressing yourself assertively yet respectfully can convey your boundaries and deter others from engaging in threatening behavior. Remember to prioritize your safety and well-being above all else. In conclusion, handling threats in prison requires a combination of awareness, strategic thinking, and interpersonal skills.

By staying vigilant, maintaining composure, building alliances, and communicating effectively, you can navigate potential dangers with confidence and resilience. Your safety and security should always be a top priority, and by following these guidelines, you can better protect yourself in a challenging environment like prison.

thirty-five
observing table etiquette

OBSERVING Table Etiquette In the intricate social dynamics of a prison environment, even seemingly minor interactions like sharing a meal at the table hold significant importance. Observing proper table etiquette can help you navigate through potential conflicts and forge positive relationships with your fellow inmates.

Here are some key points to keep in mind when it comes to dining in prison:

- **Respect personal space:** When sitting down to eat, make sure to give your fellow inmates enough space and avoid overcrowding the table.
  - Respecting personal boundaries can help prevent misunderstandings and conflicts during meal times.
- **Wait your turn:** Just like in any social setting, it's important to wait your turn when it comes to serving food or getting seconds. Being patient and considerate of others will earn you respect among your peers.
- **Use utensils properly:** While the availability of utensils may vary in a prison setting, make sure to use

them correctly and avoid eating with your hands whenever possible.
    - This shows that you are mindful of basic hygiene and etiquette.
- **Avoid wastage:** Food resources in prison are often limited, so it's important to only take what you can eat and avoid wasting food. Being mindful of your consumption not only shows respect for the available resources but also for your fellow inmates who may not have enough to eat.
- **Engage in polite conversation:** Meal times can be an opportunity to engage in light conversation with your table-mates. Avoid discussing sensitive topics or engaging in arguments during meals. Instead, focus on building positive relationships through friendly and respectful interactions.
- **Clean up after yourself:** Once you have finished your meal, make sure to clean up your eating area and dispose of any waste properly. Keeping the dining area clean and tidy shows consideration for your fellow inmates and the prison staff.

By following these simple guidelines for observing table etiquette, you can contribute to a more harmonious dining experience in prison and demonstrate your respect for others in challenging circumstances.

Remember, even in the most confined spaces, basic manners and courtesy can go a long way in fostering positive relationships and maintaining a sense of dignity.

thirty-six
respecting conversations

IN THE COMPLEX and often challenging environment of prison, one of the most crucial skills an inmate can possess is the ability to engage in conversations respectfully. How you communicate with fellow inmates, guards, and other individuals within the prison community can significantly impact your safety, well-being, and overall experience during your time behind bars.

When it comes to respecting conversations in prison, there are several key guidelines to keep in mind. First and foremost, it's essential to approach all interactions with a mindset of mutual respect.

Regardless of the circumstances that brought you to prison, treating others with dignity and courtesy can go a long way in fostering positive relationships and diffusing potential conflicts. Listening attentively is another vital aspect of respecting conversations.

By actively listening to what others have to say, you demonstrate that you value their thoughts and opinions. This can help build trust and rapport with your peers, creating a more harmonious atmosphere within the prison community.

Furthermore, it's important to be mindful of the topics you discuss during conversations. Avoid engaging in gossip, spreading rumors, or discussing sensitive or inflammatory subjects that could lead to misunderstandings or escalations. Instead, focus on topics that are neutral, positive, or constructive, such as sharing hobbies, interests, or educational pursuits.

Respecting personal boundaries is also key when engaging in conversations in prison. Be mindful of others' personal space, both physically and emotionally, and avoid prying into private matters or asking intrusive questions. Respecting boundaries demonstrates maturity and consideration for your fellow inmates' privacy and autonomy. Additionally, practicing empathy and compassion in your conversations can help foster a sense of community and support within the prison environment.

Showing understanding and kindness towards others, especially during difficult times, can create a more compassionate and empathetic atmosphere that benefits everyone involved. In conclusion, respecting conversations in prison is not just about the words you speak but also about the attitude and approach you bring to every interaction.

By treating others with respect, listening attentively, being mindful of conversation topics, respecting personal boundaries, and practicing empathy and compassion, you can contribute to a more positive and harmonious environment during your time behind bars.

thirty-seven
managing boredom

IN A PRISON SETTING, one of the biggest challenges that inmates face is managing boredom. With limited activities and a lack of freedom, it's easy to become overwhelmed by the monotony of daily life behind bars. However, finding productive ways to occupy your time can make a significant difference in your mental well-being and overall experience during your time served.

One way to combat boredom is by engaging in educational activities. Many prisons offer classes, workshops, and access to libraries that can help you expand your knowledge and skills. Whether it's earning your GED, taking vocational courses, or pursuing higher education through correspondence programs, investing in your education can not only pass the time but also enhance your prospects for a better future upon release.

Additionally, participating in creative outlets such as writing, drawing, or music can provide a much-needed escape from the mundane routine of prison life. Expressing yourself through art can be therapeutic and cathartic, allowing you to channel your emotions and thoughts into something tangible and meaningful.

Physical exercise is another excellent way to combat boredom and stay healthy while incarcerated. Whether it's jogging in the yard, doing calisthenics in your cell, or participating in organized sports, staying active can boost your mood, improve your physical fitness, and help you pass the time more quickly. Socializing with fellow inmates who share your interests can also help alleviate boredom and foster a sense of camaraderie.

Engaging in meaningful conversations, playing games, or working on projects together can make your time in prison more bearable and less isolating. Furthermore, setting personal goals and creating a daily routine can provide structure and purpose to your days, making them more manageable and fulfilling.

Whether it's reading a book each week, learning a new skill, or writing letters to loved ones, having a sense of direction can help you stay focused and motivated. Lastly, practicing mindfulness and meditation can help you stay centered and calm amidst the chaos and confinement of prison life. Taking a few moments each day to breathe deeply, reflect on your thoughts and emotions, and cultivate inner peace can make a significant difference in how you cope with boredom and stress.

In conclusion, managing boredom in prison requires creativity, resilience, and a proactive approach to finding constructive ways to occupy your time. By engaging in educational pursuits, creative endeavors, physical exercise, social interactions, goal setting, and mindfulness practices, you can make the most of your time served and emerge from prison with a renewed sense of purpose and growth.

thirty-eight
protecting correspondence

IN A PRISON SETTING, protecting your correspondence is crucial for maintaining connections with loved ones outside and safeguarding sensitive information. Letters and emails can be a lifeline to the outside world, providing a sense of normalcy and support during challenging times.

However, in a confined environment, where privacy is limited and communication is monitored, it's essential to take precautions to ensure the safety and security of your correspondence.

When writing letters or emails, it's important to remember that they may be subject to scrutiny by prison staff. Avoid discussing illegal activities, violence, or anything that could incriminate you or others. Be mindful of the language you use and refrain from sharing sensitive details that could jeopardize your safety or legal standing.

Stick to positive and uplifting messages that focus on personal growth, future goals, and maintaining relationships.

To protect your correspondence, consider the following tips:

1. **Use Discreet Language**: Avoid using coded language or discussing sensitive topics that could raise

suspicion. Keep your communication clear, respectful, and free of any incriminating information.

2. **Avoid Contraband**: Do not attempt to smuggle contraband, such as drugs or unauthorized items, through your correspondence. This could lead to serious consequences and jeopardize your safety.
3. **Secure Your Writing Materials**: Keep your pens, paper, and envelopes secure to prevent others from tampering with your correspondence or using them for unauthorized purposes.
4. **Respect Privacy**: Be mindful of others' privacy when writing letters or emails. Avoid sharing personal information about yourself or others that could compromise their safety or security.
5. **Maintain Confidentiality**: If you receive sensitive information in a letter, handle it with care and avoid sharing it with others. Respect the confidentiality of the correspondence you receive.
6. **Report Suspicious Activity**: If you notice any suspicious behavior related to correspondence, such as tampering with mail or inappropriate content, report it to the appropriate authorities.
7. **Limit Personal Details**: Avoid sharing excessive personal details or information that could be used against you. Protect your identity and maintain a level of anonymity in your correspondence.

By following these guidelines, you can protect your correspondence and maintain meaningful connections with the outside world while serving time in prison.

Remember that communication is a valuable tool for staying connected and informed, so approach it with caution and consideration for your safety and security.

thirty-nine
avoiding food risks

IN ANY ENVIRONMENT, including prison, maintaining a healthy diet is crucial for overall well-being. However, in a correctional facility, there are additional risks and challenges associated with food that must be carefully navigated to avoid potential health issues.

Here are some important considerations to keep in mind to mitigate food-related risks while serving time.

One key aspect to pay attention to is the source of the food. In prison, the origin and handling of food items may not always be transparent, so it's essential to be cautious when consuming meals. Avoid consuming expired or questionable food items, as they could lead to food poisoning or other health complications. Stick to the designated meal times and locations to ensure you are receiving food that meets basic safety standards.

Additionally, be mindful of food allergies or intolerances you may have. It's crucial to communicate any dietary restrictions or special requirements to the prison staff to prevent adverse reactions. If you have concerns about the quality or safety of the food provided, don't hesitate to raise these issues with the relevant authorities in a respectful manner.

When it comes to food preparation, hygiene is paramount.

Ensure that the food handlers follow proper hygiene practices and that the cooking facilities are clean and well-maintained. Avoid consuming food that appears to be undercooked or improperly stored, as it could pose a risk to your health.

Furthermore, be cautious when accepting food from other inmates. While sharing meals can be a gesture of camaraderie, it's essential to be aware of potential risks, such as contamination or tampering. If you are unsure about the safety of a particular food item, it's best to politely decline rather than risking your health.

Lastly, staying hydrated is crucial for your overall health and well-being. Drink plenty of water throughout the day to prevent dehydration, especially in hot or humid conditions. Be cautious of consuming sugary drinks or excessive caffeine, as they can lead to health issues if consumed in excess.

By staying vigilant and mindful of potential food risks, you can better protect your health and well-being while serving time in prison. Remember to prioritize your safety and make informed choices when it comes to food consumption to avoid unnecessary health complications.

forty
navigating guard relationships

AS AN INDIVIDUAL SERVING time in prison, navigating relationships with guards is a crucial aspect of your daily life. Interactions with guards can impact your safety, privileges, and overall experience while incarcerated.

Here are some important guidelines to help you effectively navigate guard relationships during your time in prison:

1. **Respecting Authority**: It is essential to show respect towards guards at all times. Maintaining a respectful attitude can help in avoiding unnecessary conflicts and disciplinary actions.
2. **Following Rules**: Guards are responsible for enforcing the rules and regulations of the correctional facility.
    - It is important to follow their instructions and adhere to the established guidelines to ensure a smooth and trouble-free experience.
3. **Communication**: Clear and respectful communication with guards is key. When you need assistance or have concerns, approach guards calmly and politely to address the issue.

4. **Avoiding Confrontations**: Conflict with guards can have serious consequences. It is advisable to avoid confrontations and disagreements whenever possible to maintain a peaceful environment.
5. **Understanding Boundaries**: Guards have a job to do, and it is important to understand and respect their professional boundaries. Avoid crossing lines that could lead to misunderstandings or conflicts.
6. **Reporting Issues**: If you encounter any problems or witness inappropriate behavior from a guard, report it through the appropriate channels. Your safety and well-being are important, and addressing concerns promptly is crucial.
7. **Maintaining Professionalism**: Treat interactions with guards in a professional manner. Avoid engaging in gossip, rumors, or personal conversations that could compromise your relationship with them.
8. **Following Procedures**: Guards are trained to follow specific procedures and protocols. Cooperate with them during routine checks, searches, or other security measures to demonstrate you're in compliance.
9. **Respecting Their Role**: Acknowledge the role guards play in maintaining order and security within the facility. Showing appreciation for their efforts can foster positive relationships.
10. **Avoiding Manipulation**: Attempting to manipulate or deceive guards can lead to distrust and negative repercussions. Be honest and straightforward in your interactions to build trust.

By navigating guard relationships with respect, communication, and professionalism, you can contribute to a safer and more harmonious environment within the correctional facility.

Remember that guards are there to ensure the security and well-being of all individuals in their care, including yourself.

www.ingramcontent.com/pod-product-compliance
Lightning Source LLC
LaVergne TN
LVHW050601160826
845677LV00011B/2414